THE SELECTED WORKS SERIES / NUMBER 3

OTHER BOOKS BY DAVID GITIN

Guitar Against the Wall (Panjandrum, San Francisco, 1972)
City Air (Ithaca House, Ithaca, 1974)
Ideal Space Relations (Morgan Press, Milwaukee, 1976)
Legwork (Oyez, Berkeley, 1977)

This Once

NEW & SELECTED POEMS
1965 – 1978

David Gitin

THE SELECTED WORKS SERIES / NUMBER 3

BLUE WIND PRESS / BERKELEY / 1979

Copyright 1972,1974,1976,1979 by David Gitin.

All rights reserved. No part of this book may be reproduced by any means, including information storage & retrieval systems or photo-copying equipment past present or future, except for short excerpts in critical articles, without the written permission of the publisher.

Library of Congress Cataloging in Publication Data:

Gitin, David.
    This once. new & selected poems 1965-1978.

    (The Selected works series: 3)
    I. Title.
PS3557.I8T4   811'.5'4   79-1108
ISBN 0-912652-48-9
ISBN 0-912652-49-7 pbk.
ISBN 0-912652-50-0 signed/numbered 1 of 50

Thanks to the publishers of my earlier books: Panjandrum Press, Ithaca House, Oyez, and Morgan Press. Thanks also to Ray DiPalma who ran off a few mimeo copies of "The Careens," one copy of which Richard Kostelanetz exhibited in his "Language and Structure in North America" show (Kensington Arts Association, Toronto, 1975), and another copy of which William L. Fox exhibited in his "Concrete Poetry" show (University of Nevada, Reno, 1977).

Versions of some of these poems appeared in the following magazines: Abraxas, Aldebaran Review, Amphora, Azimuth, Baloney Street, Clown War, Encore, Famous, For Now, Global Tapestry Journal, Greenfield Review, Gum, Hills, Interstate, Invisible City, Iron, Isthmus, Journal 31, Kansas Quarterly, Konglomerati, La-Bas, Mojo Navigator(e), Out of Sight, Panache, Penumbra, Pieris Japonica Press, Poetry Nippon, Red Cedar Review, Sailing the Road Clear, Stone Post Press, Telephone, The, This, Throb, Tottel's, Tractor, Tuatara, and Western Humanities Review.

Front cover montage by Tim Hildebrand. Typeset by Dave Mattingly & printed in the United States of America for Blue Wind Press, Box 7175, Berkeley, California 94707. First Edition.

CONTENTS

from GUITAR AGAINST THE WALL

New Year   12
Yer Blues   13
The Blessing   14
White on Blue   15
Guitar Against the Wall   16
In Which   17
Absolutely   18
The Shore   19
The Exchange   20
Pillowcase   21
horse ankles   22
Trilogy   23
Rampal's flute   24

from CITY AIR

John Kennedy   26
Pierce Street   27
For Carl Rakosi   28
Lonely Woman   29
Larry's Song   30
the yellow cab   31
the sea, my ignorance, waves   32
gulls on the roof   33
wise men   34
The Pipe   35
red tail-lights   36

from LEGWORK

Dreamtrack   38
Ocean   39
Table   40
a tree   41

Related to the Sea   42
Meadowlark   43
March Winds   44
The Angel Poem   48

from IDEAL SPACE RELATIONS

time out of mind   56
Umlauting   57
Ontology   58
Zeno   59
American Motors   60
Minifunk   61
The Sway of "A"   62

THE CAREENS   64

THIS ONCE

The Last Moose in Minnesota   70
Erasable Bond   71
Better Days   72
Resurrection   73
Interval   74
Stanzas from 'Two 'Three   75
Presque Rien No.1   76
No Sweat   78
Horizon (#2)   79
Buffalo   80
Congruence   81
Miles Beyond   82
Ukiah   83
Chapter   84
Gumbo Heaven   85
The Pilgrim   86
Canvas   87
Morning Song   88
A Leaf   89

Sex Paint   90
In the Wrists   91
Untitled   92
Keep Me from Blowin' Away   94
The Measure   95
The Great American Garage Sale   96
Beam   97
Letter (#2)   98
Pent Up   99
Moment's Notice   100
Greek Olives   101

FOR THE PLAYERS

All beauty, resonance, integrity,
Exist by deprivation or logic
Of strange position.
—JOHN ASHBERY

FROM

GUITAR AGAINST THE WALL

NEW YEAR

teeth
rubbed with black powder
burnt eggplant
ache with the slick
of rebirth

YER BLUES

words
bound of dread
end. the record

turns over
birth not
right for me

    world
I did not, do
not know

THE BLESSING

waters run gold with black silt
volcanic

        the yellow moon
pops between stars no matter the road

sixty cents buys ice
to keep the chicken for tomorrow

WHITE ON BLUE

birds
in
formation
one
straggling
tail
empty
sky

GUITAR AGAINST THE WALL

guitar against the wall
Maria makes a collage in the armchair
feet
or intensities away

love
        perpetual
   cognition

            the giddy overflow of form

                that we become
                    each other

the way you smile
            as I turn from this

IN WHICH

blue potatoes on the teapot
dance. the music in folds about the chair

which enfolds my flesh, layer
upon layer of cells a strand
in the fabric of the room

where what is amassed
orchestrates. bookcase
a cantus firmus and the couch

the couch is percussive (the
rhythm I make upon it) the
fluted tones of the teapot

blue potatoes

A B S O L U T E L Y

the end-all
be-all
and minus
of the other

THE SHORE

wind   splash of water
slurs   echoes

word-clouds hoisted to the sky
in God-exquisite mummery

THE EXCHANGE

Paul Bunyan
Damon Runyan

PILLOWCASE

embroidered

    roots

        Flowers.

    For you.

horse ankles
deer thighs

they say I have my mother's eyes

TRILOGY

1. MISS PHUNK

green strawband sneeze and
    termagant

        which forty ripening
        wonderful

  red red blue red
  quills must of seen

        her whats
        buts

2. SRR

dit   macumba
  sum portent les etoiles
      rag so

tray harp a train sichord
  all to all

3. O CANADA

massper longate
  mosquito saturday

    folding lake frontenac
    betelgeuse

Rampal's flute
snail froth in my ear

FROM

CITY AIR

John Kennedy

nightclerk and drunk
in the Postal Service
learns the scheme

     names
like Nova Albion
heard as "nova-albin"   a drug
past any concept of need

PIERCE STREET

a black
man staggers
as he carries
a dead
German shepherd
across his shoulders

FOR CARL RAKOSI

out
in the open air

silence
I think to call recall

from dream

chimera
the shimmer of light

where the blacktop
appears to end

curves
to continue

LONELY WOMAN

she looks
up from the tea leaves

a glance
that fears to touch

and not be
touched

in spite of which

she laughs

LARRY'S SONG

wife's
Creole

long hair down to here

I wouldn't let her
cut it

now it's white
falling out

but snow white
y'understand

my wife

the yellow cab
streaks under the
streetlight

skids to a stop
midway down the block

a man
hunched in the door
(it is raining

looks back
once

and disappears
into the fog

the sea, my ignorance, waves
and Fate in his armchair
glints sharp questions, owlish
as his wife, half-turned, addresses
the smoke, the only light, from the stove
. . . blackbellied fire . . . but she—
my wife looks
to see the terror they tap in me:
what do I believe?

Faust who does not know
his nature.
empty teacup.   they say speak
of the sea as a man who knows nothing
of the sea and ignorance
will disappear

earlier on the hill we stopped
sat on the path.
she smiles who sees many fail
the temptations her husband exposes

naked
among my books   shadows
that thirty years later I may be judged . . .

gulls on the roof
shimmer

heroic in the absence
of wonder

numbers
on the calendar

red days of increased
abandon

words a burst of
heat

like storm clouds
on radar

a white jagged border
around smooth black space

wise men
mounted in a boat the mast
gone

my name is Edward
he said
TV flickering between the words

THE PIPE

the stuff of life is mutable
agony the news of the world
recurrent as "I light my pipe"
a presumption of the poem
where the pipe is being lit
though the pipe does not light
it is the tobacco takes flame
and one wants to say with Magritte
"this is not a pipe"

red tail-lights
    passing cars

       North star
    there among the weeds

FROM

LEGWORK

DREAMTRACK

two horses

    chew the sun
        bleached grass

           and lope
                volumes of air away

OCEAN

bones of dead fish. the year

    ends. blast of light. cigarette

ashes curl   sinews of love   shadows

        blue in green

TABLE

carved pumpkin
   Mexican bowl
      full of nuts

gourd from Peru
   rings burned from the bare
      peak to the pilgrims
         at the base

white and black beans
   to play "GO"

air plant

world atlas

a tree
on the creek bank
downriver from the falls

roots
exposed

clutch stones
for balance

RELATED TO THE SEA

homage to John Marin

1

the sea
mark where the eye
collects form

black squiggles of lead mountain
red ored peaks

a village the face of sky
Deer Isle   a church   and snails

autumn trees
one two three   three one two
two one three

"paint wave a-breaking on a paint shore"

2

blue bridge
    redeye sun
        white waves on sand

a city
        automobile fish
                in a welter of coral

MEADOWLARK

through the smoke
trees
exported for timber
cities a paper world
toppled in the stream
like flesh

edge of the roof
joined by three birds
wind chimes

dance dance
to see you are spinning
for there is a pillar of salt
desire
etched upon the sky

roots of my eyes
the crust of pain or joy
refrain
to death fierce
meadowlark

MARCH WINDS

no robin at hand
  but a western meadowlark

in the clump of weeds
  to be our garden

I burn the trash, the match
  set carefully, the pack

exploded Friday when the poet
  said "Faust"

"cosmic circuit"
  in black letters on the desk

a list of little magazines, fringe
  of new consciousness

        The Modern Utopian
        S.C.R.E.W.
        Speaking of Herbs
        Artery

the space-heater   red bands
  glowing on the porch Maria
    inside with The Rainbow

distracted from the virus
  our pills and diet fail to cure
    and what of this

interlude   before I read the torn
   packet of poems sent by the girl
      from England

                        the Scientific American
               and whatever else

keeps me from the bills the tedium

a kiss on the nose
      Maria off to bed
with her nightly
         "who knows? who knows?
            nobody."

the dark absolute night
         what do I see there?
      the moon   blackness

my self staring back
         in the window

I do not fear
      the unknown
   unknowing
         but for shadows
            I name
      captive

to the vanity
      I diffuse
   so many stars
            give audience

45

books I turn to again
again to read what?

     A Nest of Ninnies
     Technicians of the Sacred
these titles

       or The White Goddess
         Epitaphs of Our Times

  Gringos and other stories.
outside

       islands of self
    challenged

          or at once someone else, object
   of my own attentions, beloved
       husband to that love
          another proffers

      never to be inside
        more skins than one

          the pupil
      of the third eye
     found wanting

"I want. I want."   knowing
    what I need to know
      subject to the unrelenting

surge of one
    self who

knows

who knows?

nobody.

THE ANGEL POEM

1

                the needle
threaded works a coat
                prayer
                                to every need

        the alcoholic Negro
            surrounded by his daughters
        in the street below

                    cries out, tries not, in his
                        drunkenness, to hurt them, cries

            as his fists blunder

    little arms
push up   out
    from her narrow shoulders &
nightgown

                    appleskin cheeks
                    starcold eyes

                    blanket
                            a spark
                in darkness

2

the tree's hump

    birthmark, turned "G"
    surname
    from "separation" "gypsy" and "song"

        limit   (Loki tricked
        to drink the horn
        empty it
        that was the ocean

outstretched arms

        Venus bone smooth
        terror of seed

    greenblack vapors
    the natal wound

I hold yr breast in a cigarette
watch the ashes curl

        to find who I am and forget

  as the sun
    penetrates my room

3

cigarette squeezed flat
cobra-headed

Mother & Nation
same root

in Hebrew–
made by God

I told Kinsey
no view

my parents' flesh
proved otherwise

old friends   ardors
that gather and pass

generation

nutrition

residue I breathe
out to the air plant

scattered
flute tones
from a puck
ered mouth

4

planets
    we choose to notice
figure
    the blue-black sky

        seventeen
        years the white
        dream shattered

        music
        the shuttle
        from lover to lover

        circle
        round the moon

                the limp
                ing man

                exposes
                the town

                and she is angry
                cries out

       intimacy
    the letters

          of friendship
          marketed

          the city
          gallery

studio walls
  lined with records

    micro
        phones and ampli
              fiers

  chamber musicians
      strive for ancient
           harmony

    violin
    violin
    violoncello
    viola

6

leaves
  animal traces

      ground on which
            we step

                  light
                  as thieves

      ocean
  relentless waves sirens

            bristle of hair
            stomach

                  cells
                  selves

            swollen mouth
  of the Russian River

7

what we devour

     biological
   justice

      our skins carried
    for future form

poems / fish

    embody
        the one
   body

      messages

      messengers

          angels

FROM

IDEAL SPACE RELATIONS

time out of mind
TV you can kiss

*

can't have
just it

*

the slope
behaves

*

man
and woman

a man with
a hat

still
life

UMLAUTING

whole

and *heal*

can be

accounted for

by umlauting

ONTOLOGY

if it's
not I

don't know
what is

ZENO

arrow
space

matter
of time

AMERICAN MOTORS

Gremlins
Sportabouts
Hornets
Javelins
Matadors
& Ambassadors

MINIFUNK

under
yonder

RAM
BLING

blunder
buss

boat a
bout

mo
raine

THE SWAY OF "A"

a life
alive all

THE CAREENS

THE CAREENS

for John Cage

(1)

creosote juniper blasé
parallax vanilla othello echelon
chthonic lozenge avuncular

tiara deciduous suture assume
technirama meridian
chesterfield spice cataract gneiss

sable juarez intricate crimson
how laser varitone melisma
buckle nouveau eschewed

(2)

coulomb toboggan Wednesday
piton violet cache oak
toggle inebriate Oregon

buxom maritime mustard sangria
endemic Taurus forest triumvirate
kremlin yachts voter

chicken Napoleon embouchure
asters crullers mahi-mahi
egregious ordinals notify

(3)

jog stound coil roost the gloss
morph venue slap soccer camph elan spumoni
spew easel fetch nak a vania ling octave
oceanal votary lug dash no spuri torque
effer om H's semble baby unch chase hello

(4)

ink sphere upland dice a roommate
kell ottawa steam fork unit if bundle
fissure cuba flat rep back set vise
by seem duct battle wish of this to

(5)

pump wob humus joint lock
Greek heels reef une sine
glisten twice

suff ackmo drabboard lathe
invi ocku mirror
etherweave tab vour itch

abit gany sud busi
prink tort ass brandy
mity go narm otli eft

bead inued ropin strike
shrive rup mediate
prim alk

(6)

ream ilt stan lick ammo matesque
aunt wax lab in lect agg rall
fig ulsive seums lum for ten

ana creak sure trugg where nous
row pave bar trickbird
limple throat plum

ompa lace me tations with oach
while dent shoulder come limin
ici what occupy fromage

stepticket swizzle king peni
float AM-cubes
hush clinic nova blue

(7)

shad tala on pock zine radi
hemp foli weather turb luid
guish freight degree rancid
lee onfi haze ripping clam dangerdom
rac everneck vine upseed tam
caribou bebe one-ruble forge

(8)

usica bo amp choco-sell
ex-phets wing chief skypores
vod jump hindtrail rasure
chisel lean acker gent lody
knot fec shemesh alco brace
emina hard cite ketch

(9)

bone ra goatness tudes claim red
sink kickpetal limit bask
corners infra blink DC door malaise sleepband

skull mall skid-hungry la
set of is all no billboard falter
miss flatpick cartoon-base celestial
north wrist onto vivial fan grit
lunch with apricot moral ice

(10)

odge terian Arizona sull cot ladies
pingpong indefinite union grave
butter john snake left noon repeat
gamma cardboard chalumeau languor envelope

hydrogen skipper gliss nagahide goes
cones adept a felt defy day zone allergy
satori hike rummage with as is bateau
shi voke lens burn collarstab horse

tingleweed fliptooth orange
moviedrone cork oz rain toy fly
short stave soak
centric hives arrow riot

THIS ONCE

THE LAST MOOSE IN MINNESOTA

xylophone confetti
streams along the bar
a slug beneath Sinatra

Make Mine Bituminous

ERASABLE BOND

the raving catfaced vagina
binds an isotope of rain

& Arthur a talent for loneliness
continues

BETTER DAYS

a beginning
but absence
Happy Days
makes itself
felt so
bells drums
alla turca
Happy Days
Happy Days
a wistful
diminuendo
you whisper
Aubergine

RESURRECTION

flag discharge

    codex of nails

        zinnias

INTERVAL

the jurors

leaned more and more

toward conviction

while watching

TV reports

on their own

deadlock

Fissure. Who threw the clock? An edge. The
steps a warp process. A coda polite?

Tone control. Enforced night.
Power postule cavity fill. An act of skin.

"Space is not a relation between substances
but between attributes." Syntax equal to dream.

PRESQUE RIEN NO. 1

inhering
a composition
by Luc Ferrari

daybreak on the beach
birds   motor   dreamtime life
suntan people exchange
in repeats
continual puncture of the world
with "I"

BA-BY   low hum   continuum
discrete activity distorts
for oneness
dredging notions of self
"constant"   "threat"

or reassurance: the temperature
Monsieur is kept constant
faithful   the constant wife
a sounding   tap the wave for occasion
a plain   /planes/

motor   cat-purr   C-A-T
spells "cat" (a creed)
no matter   song
has consequence   another song

laughter up at the front   /   of

there   /   also

DO NOT THINK   /   position

drying up   /   off

a rubbing

NO SWEAT

A handshake deal gives way to

Elf Clear Plastic Utility

Bags carried out to the street.

Alienation. Love it or leave it.

H O R I Z O N (#2)

for Michael Palmer

I do not know where I am he said
walking toward the horizon

he was walking upon the horizon
another saw

and a third saw these two
bisecting a line leading to the horizon

which was a line
imagined as final and so unseen

BUFFALO

the true condition of matter

fluid distinctions

like the isolation of favor

knitting needles in the green bag

not to think mountains

use glue at the point

bring around source connections

(closer)

(and)

what are they doing to the river?

with George Swoboda

CONGRUENCE

Expect lilac.

Sprout a cigar.

Change a menu.

Salt the stairs.

Razor and rubberband radio.

A booth on the globe.

Flatted seventh.

"This mannerism which our fear of Being

makes us accept."

Summer thumb trance.

An ad for milk.

Riddle root.

"Egoless for one pulse of the Between."

MILES BEYOND

lucid in ecstasy

cool

riddle can is

be as only

another's other?

U K I A H

SHRUB   MUTE   POINT   DWELL   RED

HAZEL   MOP   LION   ARK   LIDGE

SQUEEZE   BORN   PASS   BAND   A

CHAPTER

lefthanded mattress
   a vaudeville of doubt
      Little Benny
swaps guitarchords
         for the future

  a shade
hooked to a window
   shuts out the oak
     but think
   of the roof
it's all right

GUMBO HEAVEN

my brother the rented eye

THE PILGRIM

walkin'

contra

diction

CANVAS

spirit Drive-In
  absence proved with "you"
dumped ashes in a manzanita
cornered
  Raku baked-on drips
  peanut-butter sauce
failure of birth or thought
  ejected eighth-notes

  the lake frozen over
and fishermen drop lines
through ice

    the missing halo
  itches the mitzvah
    unimagined waves
tolling
    the pampered headache
  of high school problem shoes
    a barely-weaned promise
  the veteran cries
    "Hello flag"

MORNING SONG

220 volts AC the under
lying drone of the city

"a kind of spatial, tangible
analogue of silence"

dreams on a new mattress
global whispers

it's the aurora in me

A LEAF

A leaf
caught in the mouth

A tone
caught in silence

Breathing
the dark

News
of a difference

Shadows
thin out or accumulate

SEX PAINT

neglect

red behind general

enterprise

in only figures a bit

white-hot

and ease

extreme by such

abandon

fit valentines

couch creamy consciousness

trundling apples

IN THE WRISTS

up a waver
bikewire sphere
nails need
and April

lines liquid
unassigned
to act
some matter

the blue
rain the
silky
descents

in a word
the hang of it
not talking
and talking
something else

UNTITLED

in the generation after
all is given in pledge
the shop is open
look about   it's natural to forget
not carelessness
things coming and going
a strict account

aspirations and rejection
the medium in Paris
complex lead unflinching
'I will choose neither'
merely a coherent assemblage of sounds
and a radical:

ought labor as metaphorical as nominalism
be offered the glass?
and which is one
who was young enough to count to
seven?

always a quarrel
sterility I blame on fright
do I like it at all?
nobody told. refusal. the characters
in the hall. integrity.
the book gave the days
nothing like Italy
buying sugar that looked like champagne

a hotel and a funeral. sprayed
with gas. a way which by time
is justice:
if they fall they fall leaving
"it" the story
with "honor" your grandfather

KEEP ME FROM BLOWIN' AWAY

the blue lie
satisfied
windows torn
drive

belief?
to choose
excuses
colors run together

sunshine homilies

merciless
entropy

THE MEASURE

A Manichean etherzone fatback Max

heard as Hopi

"a double, Old Crow, on the rocks"

THE GREAT AMERICAN GARAGE SALE

      of right reason argued some
plum cotton toolkit message
  plastic vertebra, an accident, she said
of temper. the directionals, that parking lot,
  the way the rain dampens. we all do
leave, and the policecar watches
  after the movie. skin cream.

          classbound. one must
try Dorothy, erotic New Jersey levels,
  country radio will not cooperate.
(the old series, Mr. Bradley? Second Coming?)
  no deadline. as yet. seed
verified by horny reflectors. afternoon lotus

       "you learn to talk no matter
how well you plan." lunch from the union.
  combination of midwest cider and force.
in 28 years he may forget an envelope
  with an earlier date.

       the moral taunt:
your tape will be used. in memory of money.
  extension possible. like stories?
send to Affirmations, re-order contact model,
  operative. religion need not apply.

B E A M

for Ted Enslin

each difficult 'which'
a single light
boxes spring

address years some
time finely seen
no thing

ground patches
remakes accenting
emptiness

a question
switch sunsets

LETTER (# 2)

"Day's garish eye"
decor for the will

scatter of fidelities in landscape— "a Blake
lake with Byron cedars all around"

flock of blackbirds straight up
like stars leaving the flag

the hour drops free
scent of lilac

Apache decal on the windshield
a version of the way we were

stay.   on.   the.   block.
("Poetry," the Harvard graduate said

outback

the mollusc on stage at california's first theatre

PENT UP

between a training wheel

and permafrost

MOMENT'S NOTICE

it was all street
    metallic and bright gold

open windows
    terms of growing up

a lot of cobalt blue
    the image you see in a puddle

GREEK OLIVES

sites gouged to prove
enigmas walk and crawl

kiss your children
empty-handed women

oh I sat down with mirrors and chains
in the garden

I sat down
in the garden

sunrise
"all that looks bright and speaks honestly"

THE SELECTED WORKS SERIES:

(1) Light Years: Selected Early Works: Merrill Gilfillan
(2) Sojourner Microcosms: New & Selected Poems 1959-1977
    by Anselm Hollo (with a foreword by Robert Creeley &
    an afterword by Edward Dorn; author's note; index)
(3) This Once: New & Selected Poems 1965-1978: David Gitin
(4) The Selected Ted Berrigan